I0412933

Writing Your First Novel:
This is How You Do It©

By Patricia A. Toth

© Copyrighted 2015. All rights reserved - worldwide.

2017 2rd Edition

Originally published as "Writing Your First Novel: Sharing the Lessons I Learned," *Writing Your First Novel: This is How You Do It"* is non-fiction.

This book has been written, edited, designed, and published by Patricia A Toth.

No part of this book may be reproduced or transmitted in any form or by any means, electronically or mechanically, including photocopying, recording, scanning, or by an information storage and retrieval system, without the express written permission of the author, except as permitted by law.

For information or permissions, contact PatriciaAToth@mail.com.

Table of Contents

Introduction.. 7

Get Focused 9

Know Your Tools 11

Create an outline 15

Develop the Plot.. 21

Believable Characters 25

Don't Fake Reality... 32

Write it 35

Get Edited 39

Front and Back Matter 45

Letting Go 46

Thank You 47

Introduction

Authors have been writing fiction for centuries, and there are many books that will step you through the process. What you'll find here is based on what I experienced while writing my first novel. This is your opportunity to learn from someone else's experience.

Some writers believe you write your novel in your mind before committing it to paper. Close your eyes and imagine you see a tall handsome man. He looks a lot like Hemmingway and he's strolling barefoot along the seashore with the top buttons of his crisp white shirt unbuttoned and the wind is ruffling his gray hair. He stops, smiles, and softly declares, "I've done it. My novel is written. It's completed in my mind," and he rushes off to his typewriter. It's a nice picture that makes writing a novel sound really easy. It isn't. Be prepared to understand that writing a novel takes work.

There's another approach some writers like. They begin by developing the middle of the story and then they add the beginning and the end. I've tried this and my mind won't let me start in the middle. However, it might work for you.

I'm a traditionalist who believes the best approach is to develop an outline at the beginning of the process and slowly add your decisions to it, and that's what you'll find in this book. You can always try the other methods when you're about to write your third or fourth novel.

Get Focused

We all know life can come at us pretty fast. There are jobs, family, and all sorts of distractions that put demands on our time. That's why, before writing your first word, you need to set aside a time and place for writing. No matter what else is going on around you, you need to focus on your novel and only your novel. It may be an hour, two hours, or six hours a day; or it might be only once a week. Look at your life and find your place and create a schedule that works best for you.

Sometimes we can control our environment; sometimes we can't. You must be determined to carve out the time and the place where you'll do your writing. The place you find should be comfortable. It could be your office at work (after hours, of course!) or your home office with a lock on the door. If you don't have an office, consider using a table at the library, a friend's back porch, or any other place where you're alone and there are little or no distractions. Where this place is isn't important. What is important is that you are able to focus without being interrupted.

When it comes to being interrupted, there are two major sources: people and your telephone. That's why you need to talk with the people who are most likely to interrupt you. If they're little people, do your writing after you've tucked them into bed at night, or before they wake up. If they're grown-up people, explain that they must stay away unless there's a major crisis.

There were times when I found myself so deep into writing that I'd glance at the clock and, to my surprise, what felt like five minutes had actually been two hours. This is what you're striving for. So close the door. If there's a television or radio, turn it off. Also turn off your telephone. The fewer distractions you have, the easier it will be to concentrate on your novel.

Realize that you're growing this wonderful new thing that never existed before. As you progress, don't be surprised when you experience an amazing sense of accomplishment. Your determination to set aside a dedicated writing time and place will get you through to the day when you hold your published book in your hand. The good news is, by following the rest of the steps in this book, that day will happen.

Know Your Tools

I know this seems obvious, but I've been around enough writers to know there are some who think they can write, but the truth is they can't. I'm not talking about their plot or character development. They might have had a great story to tell; but I couldn't enjoy reading it. The author's poor grammar, spelling, or punctuation kept me busy trying to figure out what they meant to say. In frustration, I quit trying. You don't ever want to do that to your readers.

Words, and how you manipulate and arrange them, are your tools. You'll use them to create people and places, to evoke emotion, and to paint images in your reader's minds. Like watching an artist's brush dripping with vibrant color swirling across a canvas, your words need to paint a mental picture. Consequently, you must feel comfortable using words to tell a story people want to keep reading.

It is a great idea for you to hire an editor before submitting your manuscript for publication. However, it is to your advantage to give the editor a good quality draft. There are several types, or levels, of edit; but no matter which you choose, your editor wants your manuscript to be as well written as possible. We'll talk some more about editors and levels in another chapter. For now, it's important to understand you are responsible for using words to the best of your ability.

Your use of language does not need to be perfect. Let's face it, none of us are. However, you want to get as close to perfect as you're able. The people who buy your novel expect it to be readable. You should have a basic understanding of how to write good English - American English if you live in the United States; or British English in the UK; or Portuguese Spanish if you live in Spain; or Mexican Spanish if you live in Mexico.

Whatever your language, you need to be competent. Do you need to strive for drive-yourself-crazy perfection? No, but errors make your reader stop reading. You don't want that to happen.

Your goal is to write so your reader understands the story you are telling. A reader's attention shouldn't be interrupted by your spelling or grammar errors. These errors are like speed bumps in your reader's mind. They slow him down. After finding too many of them, and he'll stop.

You might be thinking, "So what?" He already bought my book. The answer to your question is simple. When you write and publish your second book, he'll recognize your name and remember he didn't enjoy reading your first book. Chances are good he won't buy the second book.

If you have any doubt about your skill, take a refresher class at your local high school, college, or online. You can search for help on the Web. As another alternative, visit the library and talk with a librarian. Explain what you want to accomplish and ask for recommendations.

Because writing has been my profession for more than 25 years, I turned to a friend who is a retired English teacher. She read my draft of *Beth's Diary: Such an Ordinary Day*, and then she made several recommendations that made it a much better novel. Use whatever resources you have to help improve your writing.

Another way to understand how to string words together is to read classic literature, or you can read more books about how to write or how to write good fiction. Remember, you want to focus on books that show you what good quality writing is.

It also makes sense to keep a variety of reference books handy. If you don't have good resource books on a bookshelf, you can find dictionaries, encyclopedias, and other reference materials online. Remember, it's your responsibility to write a finished manuscript with as few spelling, punctuation, and grammar errors as possible.

If you're thinking you can be a little sloppy because you'll hire an editor to fix these things, you'd be wrong. A good editor will find what needs to be corrected, but it will be up to you to make the revisions.

What happens to your novel while you are honing your writing skill? Does it grow dust in your brain because you're busy sharpening your tools? No. Not at all. You can take a class, build your reference library, or read examples of good writing; while also beginning the other steps you'll need to accomplish.

14

Create an outline

Novels begin with a creative force poking at our brains while prodding us to tell our story. Your story may come from many places. Perhaps you have a flash of inspiration, or it may be a shadowy idea that solidifies slowly. Or maybe you want to make money or become famous. No matter what your motive for writing a novel is, eventually you need to satisfy this urge by telling your story. You will want to transfer your inspiration or shadow from your mind, letting it pass through your fingertips until it can be read by others. There is only one logical place to begin: Develop an outline.

Developing an outline is the primary and most important step toward writing your novel. I can't emphasize this enough. Yes, you can read other articles that suggest you don't need an outline; but I don't agree. It's too easy to get lost on page 200 of your manuscript if you haven't planned where you're taking your reader next. So please, whatever else you do, don't skip this really important step. Your outline will keep you organized and it will keep you sane. It's the secret ingredient that makes writer's block nearly impossible.

Deciding to write your novel without an outline is like deciding to drive from Vermont to California without a map. Chances are you'll get there - eventually, but you might get sidetracked in Georgia or Oregon before finally arriving at your destination. In this case, your destination is the end of your novel. Without an outline (map), you'll waste a lot of time and effort.

Every story needs a beginning, middle, and an end, and your outline absolutely, positively must include all three. This is where you commit to how your story begins, what happens in the middle, and how the story ends. Do not begin writing if any of these three critically important elements are missing. Instead, use your dedicated writing time to think about how your story starts, what happens in the middle, and how it ends. A novel that has two of these elements, but is missing a third, will be a flop.

Now that you know your story's beginning, middle, and end, I have to assume someone already taught you how to write an outline. When it comes to outlining your novel, start at the highest level with broad descriptions.

Example: Outline for "The Widow's Stupid Son" (a working title)

Beginning	I Poor widow and son (Jack) are near starvation II Widow sends Jack to market to sell family cow III Jack is tricked into buying magic beans
Middle	IV Beanstalk grows leading to kingdom ruled by a mean giant V Jack climbs beanstalk and steals valuable stuff from the giant VI Giant chases Jack down beanstalk
End	VII Jack kills the giant and keeps the giant's valuable stuff

This outline provides the story's beginning, middle, and end. At this point, this is all you need. It tells the story in the broadest possible terms. Notice that a lot of information is missing. For example, you don't know when or where it takes place, why they're near starvation, or how old Jack, his mother, or the giant are.

You do know how the story starts, what happens in the middle, and how it ends. Like this example, the first time you write an outline you want it to be very broad.

As you progress through the other writing steps, such as plot and character development, you will return to your outline. Don't worry now about details such as tall, short, skinny, young, or elderly … active, grumpy, happy or sad. There are a zillion ways to describe people, animals, locations, situations. What you are doing with this broad outline is building a foundation. As you continue writing your novel, you also will keep adding key details to your story's outline.

If, however, you already know some or all of your story's details now, you may include them in your outline's first draft. Either way, your outline becomes a valuable tool. For example, let's say that when writing Chapter 4, you put Jack on a bus to Cincinnati, Ohio. Much later, when you're writing Chapter 7, you might not remember whether Jack is traveling by train or by bus. Will you remember if you send him to Cincinnati, Ohio, or was it Cleveland, Ohio? When you have written so many words that you can't keep track of details like these, you'll be able to refer to your outline.

We know you put Jack on a bus to Cincinnati, Ohio, in Chapter 4, but what would happen if he's on a train going to Cincinnati in Chapter 7? There's a good chance your readers will notice. That's when they'll stop reading. "A train? They might ask themselves, but wasn't he on a bus?" What will your readers do next? For one thing, if they find too many errors they won't recommend your novel to other readers.

Recently, I was reading a novel where the hero was bleeding profusely from being shot in the left shoulder. Two pages later, still bleeding, and in intense pain, he's dragging a 120-pound woman across a parking lot using the same arm. I closed the book and doubt that I'll open it again.

On the other hand, there will be some readers who will be curious about your mistakes. They not only stop reading, they also start searching for the original chapter, page, and paragraph that told them whether Jack got on a bus or a train. They want to know if they remembered correctly or if you made a mistake. Either way, you've taken them away from the story you're telling. If they have to back-track more than once, they may tell their friends not to bother reading your novel. To help ensure you're writing a book people recommend to others, keep adding important details to your outline.

While writing my novel, I found myself asking a lot of questions that only I could answer. You'll be doing the same thing. Did I say her hair was strawberry blonde or a deep auburn? Blue eyes or hazel? It was a constant effort to not only get words on the page, but also to remember what I had already written. I found myself asking questions such as "Have I mentioned this character before? Does the reader know anything about this character? Do they need this information?

I referred to my outline constantly. I kept asking and answering my own questions. Then, I recorded my decisions in the outline. If I didn't find an answer I needed in the outline, I was forced to re-read pages and more pages of my manuscript until I found the answer. If I didn't find an answer in the manuscript, I made one up. Then I made a point of adding it to the outline so I'd be able to find it quickly if I needed it again. Reading the chapters you've written to find a small piece of information really kills time.

How many details are enough or too many? It depends on your story and how you choose to tell it. No matter how many details you develop, it's important for you to keep track of them on your outline. What's beautiful is that you're writing fiction. Until your novel is published, you are the only person who knows the answer to your questions.

Your outline is a reference tool for your use only. The rule of thumb is that, if there's a good possibility you'll need to remember something you wrote, include it in your outline. By the time I finished writing my manuscript, I had more than 60,000 words and 18 chapters to sort through. However, my outline was less than a page long. How much you include in your outline is a matter of knowing your memory and your story.

Develop the Plot

The fourth step in writing your soon-to-be award-winning, outrageously successful first work of fiction is developing your story's plot. But what is a plot and why does your story need one? Think of **plot** and **plan** as being the same thing. You already started plotting your story when you created your broadest outline.

Your finished manuscript will have a beginning, middle, and an end that will match the broad outline. Yes, you may change one of these three elements while writing the manuscript, but then you need to revise your outline to match.

Have you noticed that there's a pattern? As you grow your novel the outline, manuscript, paragraphs, and sentences will all have a beginning, middle, and an end.

As authors writing fiction, we call the beginning of your novel the "**introduction**." The middle is known as "**development** (or rising action)." The end is called the "**climax**." When plotting your story, you might conclude with a **denouement,** which is simply a paragraph or several pages that tie up any loose ends.

In your outline, you began developing your story's plot. Now, while developing the plot, is when you make the more detailed decisions that tell your story. Your plot needs a **protagonist**, which is writer's jargon for "main character." This is your hero or heroine regardless of sex or species.

A story without conflict is boring, so your plot needs **conflict**. The more conflict you write into it, the more interesting it will be. It makes your readers wonder what's going to happen next. It entertains them, and it keeps them reading. If you write a chapter without conflict, throw it away. Ok, I hear you objecting. Your novel is your labor of love; but if you plan to sell it, it's also a product.

Chapters with zero conflict become a product no one wants to buy or read. Six pages that describe a location might seem important, but they'll put your readers to sleep it there's no conflict. A list of the contents of the protagonist's apartment might seem important; but without conflict, it's simply boring. You can do either of two things: Add conflict, or delete that chapter.

As you develop your plot, remember that your protagonist must have a problem. Maybe he, or she, is struggling with something or someone, or has to overcome an obstacle. Now is when you decide what the story's central conflict is and how it will be resolved. This is important: By the time your reader reaches the end of the story, you must resolve the protagonist's conflict.

In addition to the story's main conflict, you want to add a lot of lesser conflicts. They help move the story along. These smaller conflicts do not have to be hugely dramatic; however, they need to be interesting. Do your best to write conflict into every chapter; and when possible, into every paragraph.

Action must have a reaction. Ask yourself specific questions. Who is doing what, when, and who is it being done to? Where is the story taking place? What is the relationship of one character to another?

Here's an example of how action results in reaction:

> **ACTION**: Joey is a puppy chewing on his owner's slipper; Coco is a cat sleeping under the bed; and Mike is wondering where he put his slipper.
>
> These are three characters and three actions (Joey/chewing, Coco/sleeping, and Mike/wondering). Now consider possible reactions.
>
> **REACTION**: Mike finds Joey chewing on his slipper. He reacts by spanking Joey. The puppy reacts by dashing under the bed. The sleeping cat is startled by the unexpected arrival of the puppy and runs out from under the bed.

When deciding on plot actions and reactions, also consider the timing of each. The Jack/Coco/Mike example could be written as one paragraph, or as three separate events told in three different chapters. Once you've decided, be sure to include the actions/reactions in your outline.

No matter what, you must entertain the person reading your book. Never forget that it is a critical component of plot. You want people to enjoy reading what you've imagined. Give them a reason to laugh or cry, or to feel fear or joy, or all of the above. Take them to places and into situations outside of the routine of their daily lives. It doesn't make any difference if you're writing a children's book, suspense, chick lit, a murder mystery, or any other genre. As you decide on your story's plot, remember that the primary purpose of your book is to entertain your reader.

If you haven't already done so, this is as good a time as any other to give your novel a working title. Trust me; you tired of referring to it as "my book" or "my novel." Make it a title you really like, but don't fall madly in love with it. Book titles are always subject to change up until the book is published. If you publish through the traditional publishing house, chances are your publisher will change it to something experience tells them will help generate sales. However, if the title is really, really good, they might keep it.

If you plan to self-publish online, enter the title in several search engines before deciding to use it. You might find that someone else already has published a book with the same title.

By this place in the process, you've accomplished a lot. You've found your place to write, set aside time to write, developed an outline, decided on the elements of the plot, and come up with a working title.

Review your outline and make sure you've noted all of your plot's elements. Make sure you have an introduction, story development, and climax. Be sure to note any actions and reactions that must be included. All you need is enough description to help you as you're writing the story. However, you are not ready to start writing; not yet. You still need to define your characters and, quite possibly, do some research.

Believable Characters

Creating characters is fun. It's the only way to make people without having sex. You begin with nothing except a blank page (or monitor); and then you think about the people who will populate your story. Having already developed an outline and the plot, you have a good idea who your characters are. Now you're going to make them real by deciding what they look like, how they sound, and their unique mannerisms. Again, the amount of detail you need depends on the character and its role in telling your story.

It's true that nobody's perfect. Not only that, but boring characters become boring reading. Your characters need to have flaws. Even a courageous hero who just rescued a child from a burning building is more interesting if he's a pigeon-toed vagrant who has bad breath. It is your job is to give life to characters who are so real your readers forget they're reading fiction.

If you doubt the importance of your characters, consider Huckleberry Finn, Scarlett O'Hara, and Harry Potter. Were any of them actual flesh and blood people? These are the type of characters you need to develop. They grab hold of the reader's imagination because they are vividly and imperfectly human.

How do you instill a sense of humanity? Close your eyes gently and begin by visualizing your protagonist. Do you see a man or a woman? How tall? How old? Curly hair or straight? What race and what nationality? With your eyes still closed, let your protagonist move and speak. Do you hear an accent? Does he, or she, mumble or use slang? On a Sunday morning, does your protagonist go to church or prefer to sleep in? Are you creating a person who is honest or dishonest, or somewhere between? Keep asking questions until you find yourself thinking about your character as though he or she really exists. Because you believe, your readers will believe too.

Would you like to have some fun? Still thinking about your protagonist, change his/her physical characteristics and personality. If your protagonist is a female, what would happen to your story if you change the protagonist to a man? If your protagonist is a native New Yorker, how would it affect your story if your protagonist was born in China? Try imagining the protagonist as being in a different age group. By asking and answering these types of question, you are creating characters your readers will want to know more about.

Use this process of thinking about and asking yourself questions until you have created all of the characters. As the only person who knows the story you're telling, it's up to you to decide how many characters and how much information your reader needs to know.

It's a good idea to set up a simple Character Chart where you keep track of important details about each character. I keep mine on the same page as my outline. It's a great resource for finding specific descriptive information easily, instead of reading every page you've already written. Keep your notes simple.

Some of your characters don't need to be as fully developed as others. You decide this by asking yourself two important questions: "What does this character contribute to the story?" and "What does my reader need to know about the character?" If there isn't a reason for being in your story, get rid of that character.

I've written two paragraphs to help you understand. Notice the character's action and reaction in the following paragraphs. In the first paragraph, the teen triggers a specific thought in the main character's mind. Because the teen will never appear again, you don't need more description.

> "I walked passed a teenager on my way to the diner. I'm not sure if the teen was male or female because it was wearing a hoodie, pulled forward to hide the occupant's face. Why do our kids think they need to hide their faces?"

Let's look at the same teenager with more detail and how the protagonist reacts. This time the teen will appear in a later chapter.

> "I walked passed a shadowy figure almost hidden in the darkened doorway, a streetlight faintly outlining expensive tennis shoes. Appearing to fill the doorway and shrouded in a black hoodie, I don't want to know if it is male or female. I quicken my pace, not realizing I will meet this strange apparition soon."

For the first paragraph, you don't need to record the teenager on your Character Chart. His only purpose was to trigger the main character's thought, and he will never appear again. However, for the second example, you would enter notes about the teenager on your Character Chart because he continues to be in the story. You might make a note such as "Chapter 2-Johnny Guerrero. 15 years old. Illegal immigrant. Black hair and blue eyes."

Enter each character's full name in the first column, their description and statistics in the second column, and notes about personality and relationships in a third column. When I needed to remember what I had written in an earlier chapter, this chart saved me countless hours of scrolling through pages and chapters.

As another example, I created a character named Maddy. She's in almost every chapter of my novel, "Beth's Diary, Such an Ordinary Day." Maddy has hair "the color of eggs scrambled with cream." When I was about three-quarters of the way into writing the manuscript, I needed to remember what, if anything, I had written about the color of her hair. I found the answer in my Character Chart, saving me from having to read through 55,000 words.

When adding a character to your chart, keep your notes simple. If you find it helpful, you also can set up a chart for places and things. You might record information such as the color of a car or the town where someone is born. Be careful you don't overdo it by entering an excessive amount of detail. You want to spend your time writing your manuscript and not piling excessive details into an outline and charts.

Example: Character Chart

Character	Description	Personality/Other
Protagonist: James T. Hallmon	5-foot 11-inches tall, 180 pounds, bluish-green eyes, brown hair silvery at temples 56 years old, married twice, wears glasses, Slender. T = Turner – middle name he doesn't like	Intelligent, highly stressed, holds in own anger, non-combative, keeps finding own strength. Hates Jennifer but can't let go of her memory Chapter 3 "almost 20 years of being a damn good cop"
Jennifer Amelia Whitman	Jim's first wife. 5' 10" tall, skinny, hair is short, black, and curly. Died at 26.	Pregnant with Buddy's child when she died
Johnny Guerrero	Illegal immigrant. 15 years old. Black hair and blue eyes. Infectious laugh. Shy - tends to look at the sidewalk	Jim hires Johnny as handyman Amelia teaches him English. No one knows he already knows English. Really a 23 year old undercover Narc

Did you notice, when reading the character chart, that you found key elements of the plot? The chart also helps you to keep tract of the character's relationships with each other.

Don't Fake Reality

When someone begins reading your book, they want to trust you. No matter how wild your fiction is, they want to be absorbed by and believe in what they're reading. They immerse themselves in the world you've created so your plot, your characters, and your story's actions and reactions become real.

Never assume your readers are dumb. If you fake information instead of taking the time to learn the facts, you'll lose your readers. When they realize you've deceived them, they will never believe in or trust you again. They won't buy your next novel. They won't recommend it.

As the author, it is your responsibility to be accurate. When a place exists or an event actually occurred, your description needs to be correct. For example, if your characters are taking a taxi from East 40th Street to the center of downtown Manhattan, find out if there is an East 40th Street and where the center of downtown Manhattan is in relationship to it. You might learn that East 40th Street **is** downtown Manhattan, so why would your characters take a taxi to where they already are?

In my novel, I describe the parking lot of an Indian reservation and Mission in Southern Arizona. I visited the Mission in 2001, and I returned there for a second visit in 2005. During those years the parking lot and some small out-buildings changed. Any one of thousands of visitors to the Mission will recognize if I described them incorrectly.

Consequently, I needed to be certain my description matched the timeline of my story.

Let's imagine you want to describe a small town near the city limits of Chicago. Before spending time researching this town, consider its importance in your story. If the town really exists, decide how much your reader needs to know about it. If this town is important to your story, you must do the research.

There are many resources available to you. You might be lucky enough to interview someone who was born and raised there. Whether you use your local library, the Internet, visit a location, or speak with knowledgeable people, research can be fun and interesting. Doing it has the bonus of providing additional facts and descriptions to include in your manuscript and that will make your fiction more believable.

Are you writing science fiction? Let your imagination go wild, but remember you're creating what the reader will perceive as being facts. Don't contradict yourself.

Write it

Until now, you've used your dedicated writing time to do everything except write, but that's about to change. Before moving on, take a minute to congratulate yourself. You've done the hardest part of the work. You know the "who, what, when, and where" of your story, your characters are real, their actions and reactions make sense, and the conflicts and resolutions are in your outline. Your important decisions are made.

I can't tell you how many times I wrote the first half of my book. I mean that literally. I don't know the answer. I would write a paragraph or a chapter, read it, and then I'd make changes. I always saw sentences and paragraphs that could be worded better, written more tightly, or needing more description. I struggled for months, always feeling as though I was running on a treadmill, but not really getting anywhere. Then I realized what I had to do. From then on, I wrote my manuscript using a two day method.

On the first day, I sat in front of my keyboard and turned off my mind. I had my outline and character chart. I knew my plot and characters, and I had done my research. All that was left was for me to tell the story; and so I sat there and typed. I didn't think about anything other than telling the story. To heck with proper grammar, punctuation, and spelling. I had a great time playing with words. I didn't go back and re-read what I had just written. I simply kept words flowing until I was too tired to keep writing. It was wonderful.

On the following day, I read what I had written. This time I allowed myself to read critically. I corrected spelling, grammar, and punctuation. I rewrote anything that needed to be changed. Surprisingly, the previous day's work was always better than I expected it to be.

Using this two day method was so much easier than writing and editing at the same time, and it saved countless hours. Day-after-day, I repeated this process until the manuscript was completed. Perhaps you write on Monday, Wednesday, and Friday mornings. Then you review and revise on Tuesday, Thursday, and Saturday evenings. Whatever you decide on, keep on schedule.

In your entire novel, there really is one sentence that is more important than any other sentence. It is the first sentence of the first chapter. It doesn't have to be the first sentence you write, but when you do write it, it must be wonderful. This sentence is known as the **hook**. It must hook your reader into wanting to read more. If it doesn't, it might be the only sentence he or she reads. Your book's cover art is the first hook. Your book's first sentence is the second hook. Together, both hooks help a possible reader decide whether or not to buy and read your novel. The first paragraph is the third hook.

As you write, don't worry about word count. Keep writing until you believe your manuscript is finished. As a new author, chances are you'll write far too many words. Much later, when you're editing your manuscript, you will delete entire paragraphs or pages. Remember your words are tools. Don't fall in love with them. Never be afraid to throw them away when they're not needed.

Help your reader by writing short sentences. Whenever possible, write short paragraphs. Avoid clichés. Avoid run-on sentences. Pay attention that you're not unnecessarily repeating yourself.

Dialogue is a wonderful tool for moving your story forward. Use it to break up long pages of prose. When writing dialogue, be real. Because we speak much more casually then we write, don't worry about your characters using proper grammar. Let their personality show through their words. One way to learn how to write good dialog is by simply listening to the people around you. When in a group, listen to not only what they're saying, but also to how they're saying it. Observe their body language and how they express emotion.

Flashbacks take your reader backward in time. They usually provide useful information that will help your reader understand what's happening in the present. They are complex and difficult to write, and many experts recommend a first time author avoid using them. "Beth's Diary: Such an Ordinary Day" includes many flashbacks; however, I never would have attempted using them if I didn't already have five writing awards. For me, it was a fun exercise. For anyone with less writing experience, I strongly recommend you write a few novels without them before attempting flashbacks.

If you haven't already done so, this is a good time to name your chapters. If you followed it, chances are the original broad outline provides chapter headings. It's best to keep the headings short and descriptive. You want each title to reflect the content without giving the story away. Similar to the hook sentence you wrote at the beginning of the novel, the chapter titles help make your readers curious by bringing them into the story.

Congratulations. You've done your work and you're welcome to refer to yourself as an author or novelist. But don't get too excited. You're not finished. Before submitting your manuscript to an agent or publisher, it needs to be edited.

Get Edited

You love your characters and their story. Writing it was work, often hard work; but it's been fun too. You've crafted and shaped your manuscript onto pages to be printed, bound, and shared: literally or online. Eventually it will be read by others; hopefully by many others. You have every right to be proud of what you've accomplished. However, before sending your creation into the world, you have one more step. You must intentionally subject your work to criticism. Remember, the criticism is not about you. It's about your manuscript and your manuscript is not you. Because you want it to be the best story you are capable of publishing, you must separate yourself from what you've written.

Have you heard the old saying about "not seeing the forest because of the trees"? With a manuscript, you don't see what's wrong because you've been deeply immersed in writing. By now you know your story so well you don't see the problems; and I can assure you, there are problems. You must allow others to find fault. It is important that you do not take the criticism personally. Remember what I said about not falling in love with the words you've written? When it comes to criticism, you also need to remember the criticism is not about you. It is about the tools (words) you've chosen and how they're strung together.

Unless you hired a developmental editor, you begin by self-editing. There are some experts who recommend you read your manuscript aloud, using your ears to pick up any incorrect or misplaced words or phrases. This works a little, but what happens if your ear hasn't been trained to hear good grammar? Besides, your ear doesn't know the difference between a colon or a semi-colon, or "your" and "you're." There are better ways to self-edit.

To begin, put your manuscript on a shelf and don't look at it until it's covered with dust. If it's a file saved on your computer, it can't actually gather dust, so consider my remark metaphoric. Either way, my point is the same. You want enough time to pass that, from when you finished your manuscript until you begin self-editing, you feel like you're reading it for the first time. Actually, a week should be enough time.

Begin by finding and correcting misspelled words.

Find really long sentences. Shorten them. If you're using a computer, search for "and." Read what's written before and after "and." Chances are good you can rewrite one sentence as two shorter sentences.

Find the many forms of the verb "is." This includes "are" and "was" and "were" and "will be." Highlight all of them. You will be amazed by how many you find, so don't let the multitude overwhelm you. Your objective is to replace every one with a more descriptive or more active verb. (Remember those reference books I suggested? This is a good time to use them.)

- Search for "that." In many sentences, it's useless. When useless, delete it.

- Do the same thing with adverbs and adjectives ending in "ly."

- Find "have" and "got." They don't belong next to each other in the same sentence. Like "that," the word "got" is generally useless. When useless, delete it.

Ask for and accept constructive criticism from others. Let go of your ego and find a close friend or relative who you trust to be brutally honest. Ask them to tell you everything they didn't like about your story. Whatever you do, don't get angry when they tell you. You become a professional by separating yourself from what you've written.

Recognize that you need to know what must be corrected. Also recognize you don't have to revise every fault your friend or an editor finds. Think about each criticism and decide how changing it will affect your story.

For example, my manuscript attracted an agent who wanted to represent it if I would change a character who was one of my main characters. The agent didn't like the character's sloppy speech pattern. It irritated her. I strongly believe the way this character speaks helps define who she is. I felt strongly that changing her would be detrimental to the story. The agent and I went our separate ways. I made a good decision because everyone who reads my novel loves to hate this character.

Regardless of who is editing – yourself, a friend, or a professional editor, remember everything you've written is about entertaining your reader.

If you decide to retain the services of a professional editor, be sure to do ask for references. Also ask questions about the process, and negotiate. Editors typically offer three levels of edit that can include anything from their recommending extensive rewriting of your entire manuscript to their simply making suggestions that will add polish to your finished manuscript.

Editors come in all sizes and shapes and degrees of competency. When deciding who to hire, don't be intimidated. Clearly define what level of edit you're paying for, and what each of you expects from the other.

There are many types of editors and levels of edit; however, the most commonly used for a manuscript are **developmental**, **substantive**, and **copyediting**. In my eBook "Understanding Editors and Editing" I talk about the different types of editor and how each can help you.

A developmental editor works with you before you begin writing your manuscript. This type of editor helps you shape your manuscript beginning with your outline or a rough draft. You work together as collaborators. While you focus on writing content, a developmental editor helps guide the story. He concentrates on the form and provides feedback.

Substantive editors are sometimes called manuscript editors. You hire a substantive editor when your manuscript is finished. They evaluate your entire novel by looking for flaws in your writing style, the story's structure, accuracy of researchable facts, and your novel's overall tone. They find any weaknesses that when corrected, will result in an improved manuscript. Substantive editors rewrite, revise, add or delete words, and resolve anything that needs to be corrected before returning your manuscript to you.

A substantive editor should be willing to explain any revisions he or she wants you to make, and submits a final copy for your review. I recommend you keep a copy of your original manuscript in case you disagree with or are not satisfied with the revisions made by the substantive editor.

A copy editor varies from a substantive editor. A copy editor focuses on your manuscript line-by-line instead of looking at the manuscript as a whole. When negotiating for this type of edit, the copy editor and you need to decide if the copy editor will perform a light, medium, or heavy edit.

I know of a woman who refers to herself as a substantive editor; when in reality, she functions as a developmental editor. Again, I caution you to define the details of your work relationship and expectations before actually retaining an editor's services. If during an interview you discover an editor doesn't know the difference between the levels of edit, you may not want to hire him or her.

I realize you will be able to do only what your wallet or savings account allows. Regardless of the type or level of edit you use, the result is you will have the best manuscript you are capable of creating.

Front and Back Matter

Novels have what's known as front matter and back matter. These are the pages you find in the front of a book like a Title Page, Forward, Acknowledgement, Copyright, and Table of Contents. The back matter might include an Index, About the Author, or a page with a list of other novels you've written along with your Web site and/or email address.

Your editor or publisher will guide you in deciding which pages you need to include. If you don't have a publisher or editor, this is where you'll find yourself doing a lot more reading. Open a dozen or two books and study its' front and back matter until you understand the various pages.

Letting Go

Thank you for buying and reading "Writing Your First Novel: This is How You Do It." Now that you've written your story, it's time to let go. However, you're not really finished. Your book is about to become a marketable product.

Once your book is ready to be sent into the world, you will be faced with entirely new decisions. If you don't have an agent, do you need one? Should you find a traditional publishing house, or will you self-publish?

Before your manuscript becomes a solid book that a reader can hold (or view on a screen), you need to understand a mountain of information about publishing and marketing. If you have an agent and publisher, they'll guide you to stardom. However, if you self-publish and want your book to sell, it's time to visit the library again, take more classes, or Google these topics. You have two new worlds to explore and, hopefully, master: online publishing and marketing.

Thank You

I hope your novel is a fabulous success and that it reaches the stratosphere of many best-seller lists.

I also hope I've helped you by sharing what I experienced while writing "Beth's Diary: Such an Ordinary Day." If you'd like to learn more about editing your novel, I've also written "Writing Your First Novel: Hire an Editor or Self-Edit?" which also is on Amazon.com.

Your opinion matters. Amazon reviews help others decide if they'd like to read this book. If reading this book has helped you, please take a minute to leave a review.

About the author

I was born in Cleveland, Ohio, and no, I'm not going to mention the year. Let's just say I'm mature enough to have worked as a Communications Consultant and Technical Writer for more than twenty-five years. My work has been published both nationwide and globally and I've earned numerous awards.

When I decided to retire, I knew I'd continue writing. As both a senior technical writer and the author of fiction, I hope my books provide you with the help you are seeking.

More books by this author

Some of the books I've written are available as eBooks and some are both eBooks and paperback. Enter "Patricia Toth" in Amazon.com's search bar. You will find ten cookbooks, a novel, a collection of short stories and quips, and several non-fiction "how to" titles.

Have you always wanted to write a book, but you are unsure about how to do it? These books will guide you through the process of becoming a successful author. They include:

- Writing Your Life Story: It's All about You!

- Writing Your First Novel: Hire an Editor or Self-Edit?

- Technical Writing For People Who Aren't Technical Writers

Each cookbook in the **Cooking for Potlucks** eBook series includes a collection of delicious recipes. There's a cookbook for Bread, Breakfast, Cookies and Brownies, Cake, Casseroles, Chicken, Salad, Soup, Side Dishes, or Vegetables.

Do you like to read fiction for enjoyment? You will find two more books on Amazon.

- **Beth's Diary: Such an Ordinary Day** – This story is about a woman who's trying to avoid being murdered. Is she a victim or a survivor?

- **God and Odd Stories** – Experience a smile or an "awe" moment when you read this little book. You will discover a little bit of everything starting with a Christian creed, letters to God, poetry, and several short stories.

Please take a minute to write a review on Amazon.com about "*Writing Your First Novel: This is How You Do It.* Your comments will help others to decide if this book will help them too.

www.PatriciaToth.com

www.ingramcontent.com/pod-product-compliance
Lightning Source LLC
Chambersburg PA
CBHW032033290526
45786CB00012B/2662